THE SIMPLE PAPER AIRPLANE BOOK FOR KIDS

NATURESCAPE
PUBLISHING

PLANE #1

1. FOLD IN HALF, THEN UNFOLD

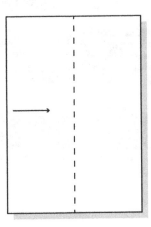

2. FOLD CORNERS TO CENTER

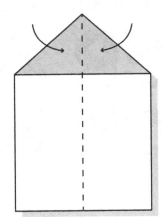

3. FOLD POINT DOWN

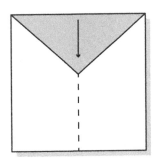

4. FOLD CORNERS TO CENTER

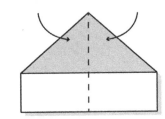

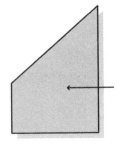

5. FOLD IN HALF

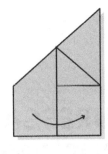

6. FOLD DOWN WINGS

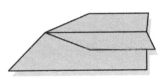

SPACE

FUN FACT

You can fit over 1,000,000 earth's inside the sun.

FUN FACT

The number of galaxies estimated in the universe is 2,000,000,000,000 (2 trillion)

FUN FACT

The earth is approximately 4,500,000,000 (4.5 billion) years old.

FUN FACT

There are more stars in space than all of the grains of sand in the world.

FUN FACT

Space is a very cold place at -270°C. (degrees celcius)

PLANE #2

1. FOLD IN HALF

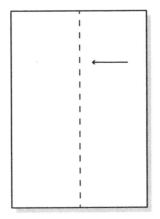

2. FOLD CORNERS IN

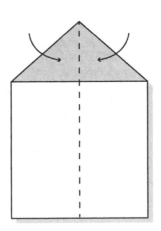

3. FOLD IN HALF AGAIN AND FOLD DOWN WINGS

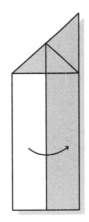

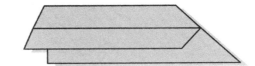

CARS

FUN FACT

The average car has over 30,000 (30 thousand) parts.

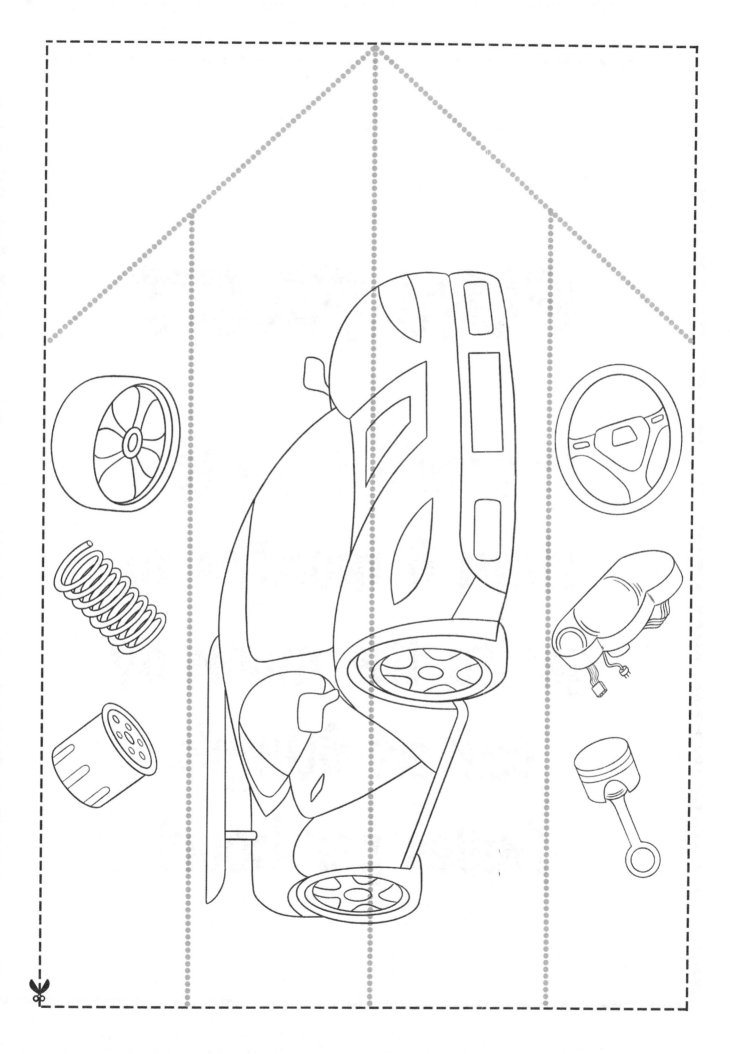

FUN FACT

It would take less than 6 months to get to the moon by car at 60mph. (miles per hour)

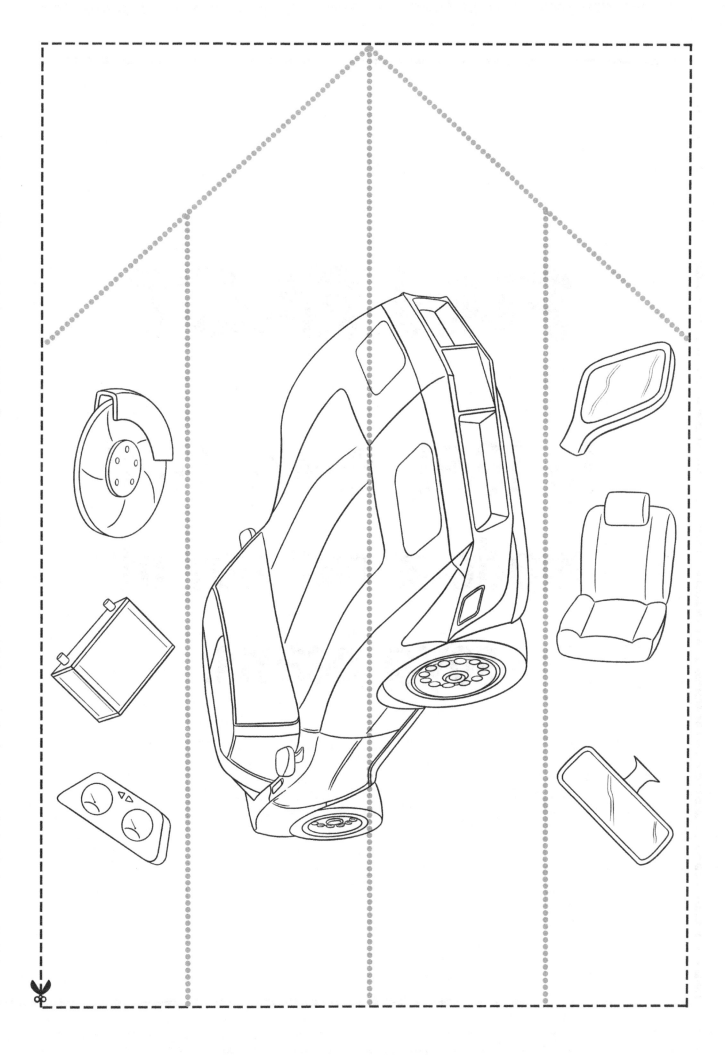

FUN FACT

In 1941, Henry Ford made a car out of soya beans.

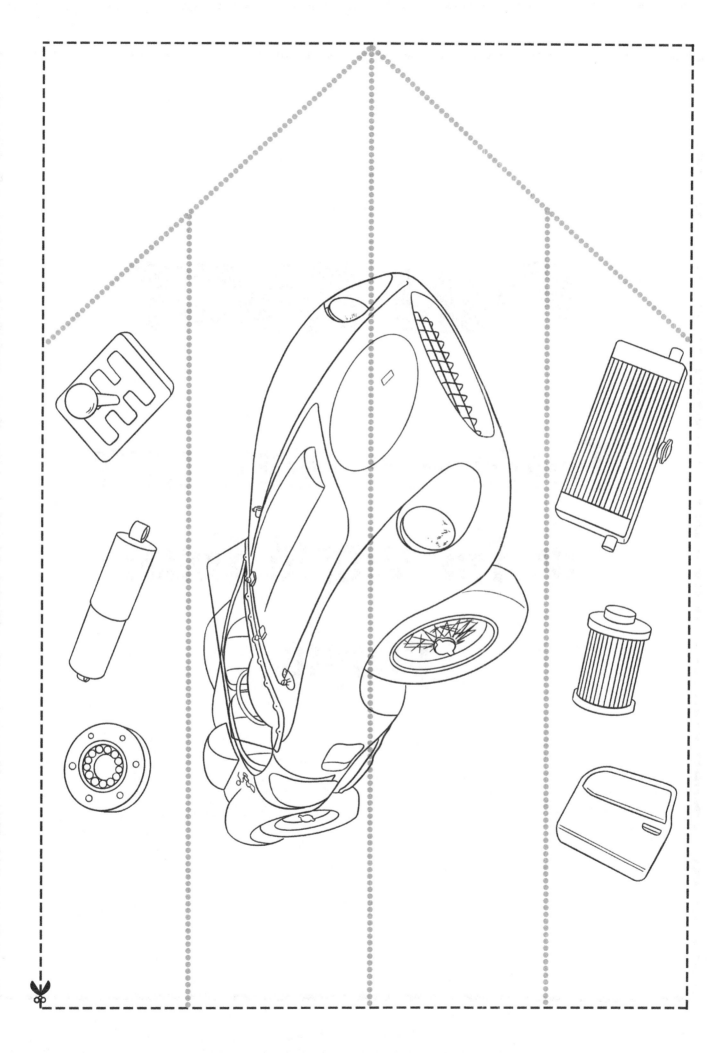

FUN FACT

There are more cars in the world than people.

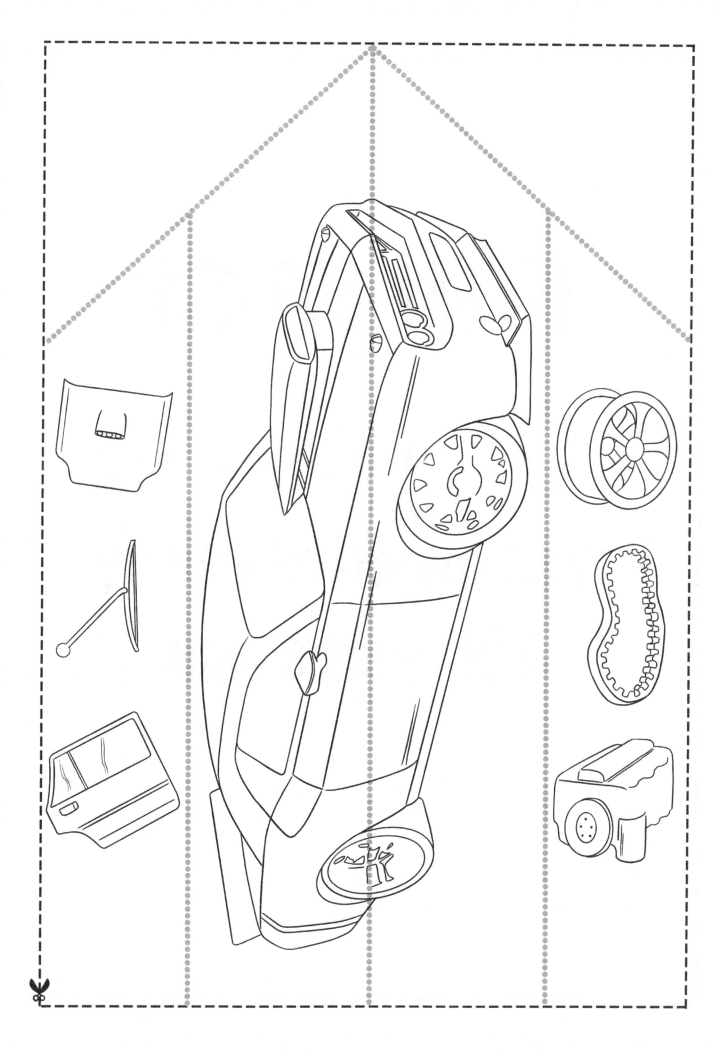

FUN FACT

The first electric car was invented nearly 200 years ago.

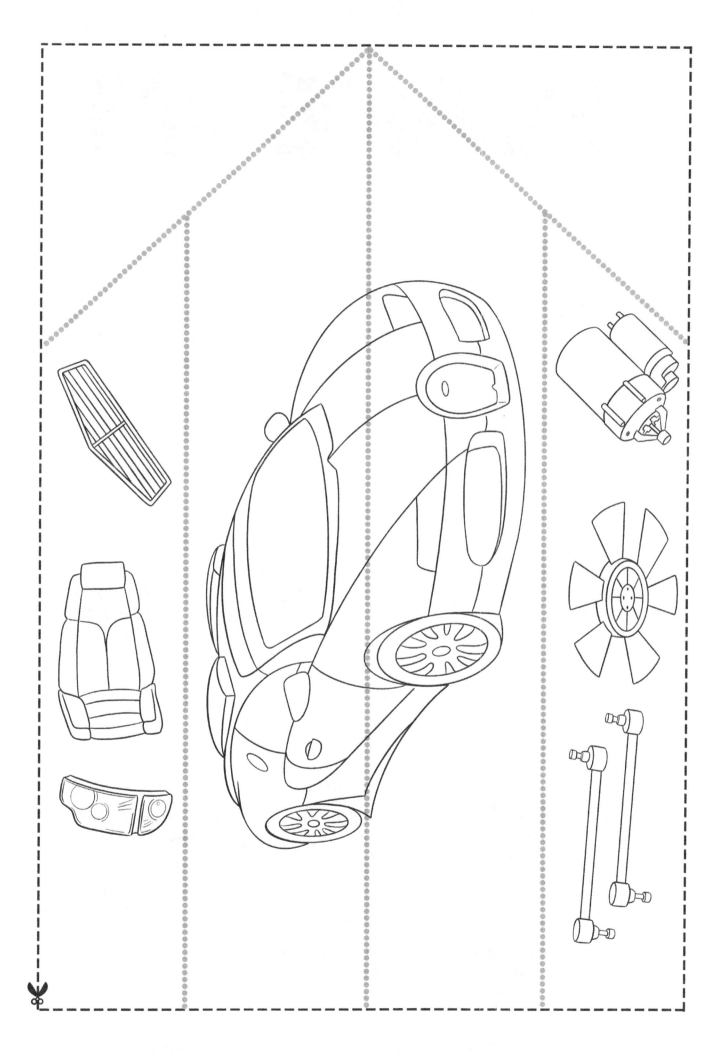

PLANE #3

1. FOLD IN HALF,
   THEN UNFOLD

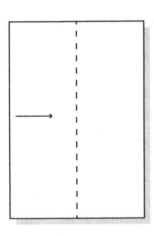

2. FOLD CORNERS
   TO CENTER

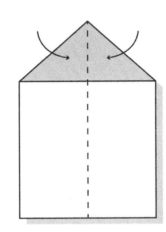

3. FOLD POINT
   DOWN

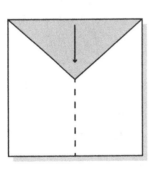

4. FOLD CORNERS
   TOWARD MIDDLE

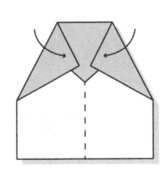

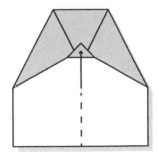

5. FOLD POINT
   UP

6. FOLD IN HALF &
   FOLD WINGS
   DOWN

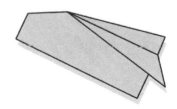

DINOSAURS

FUN FACT

Ankylosaurus lived
68,000,000
(68 million)
years ago.

FUN FACT

The weight of a Brachiosaurus has been estimated between 30 and 45 tons.

FUN FACT

Spinosaurus weighed up to 20 tons, roughly 3 elephants.

FUN FACT

A Stegosaurus's brain was the size of a ping-pong ball.

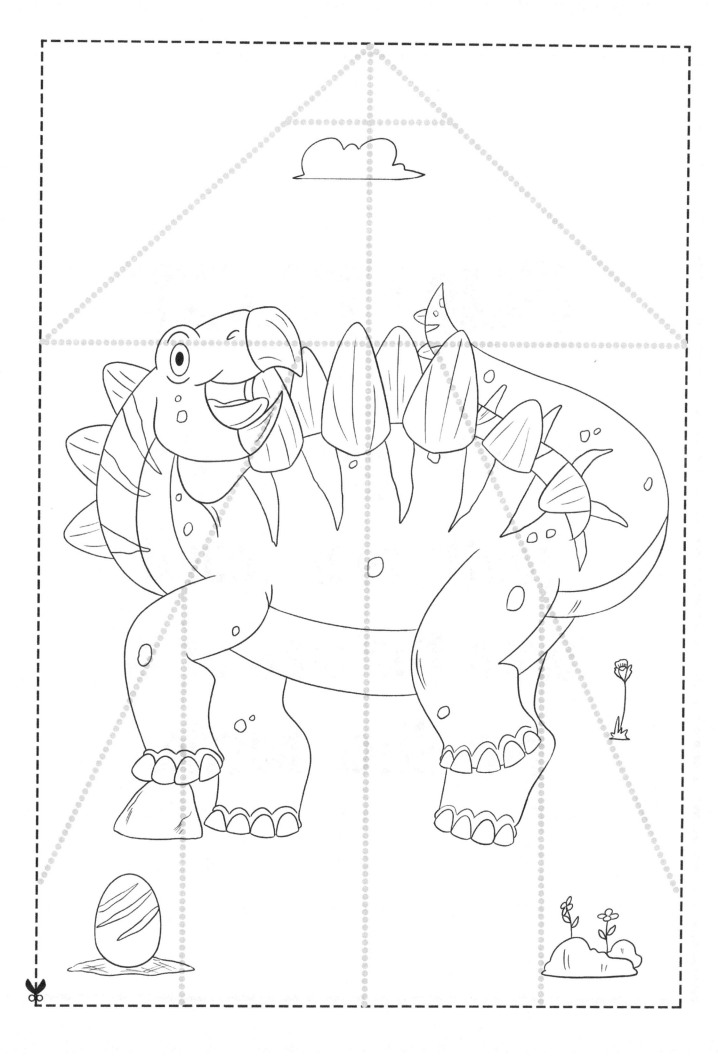

FUN FACT

The largest T-Rex tooth ever found was the size of a two-liter bottle.

PLANE #4

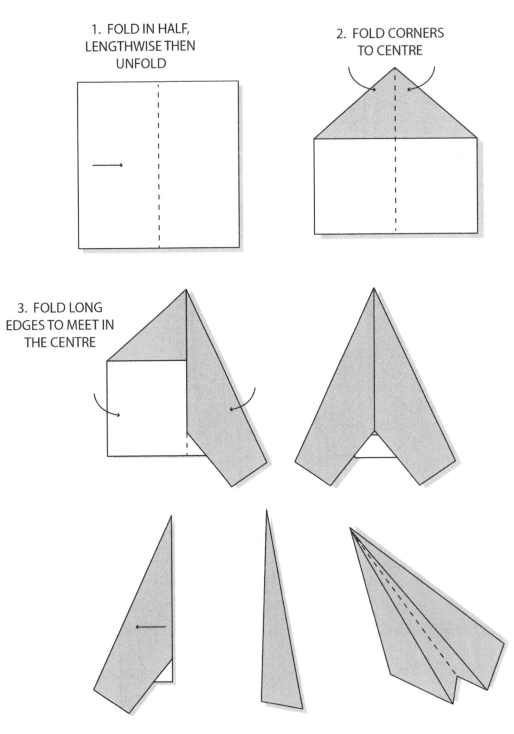

1. FOLD IN HALF, LENGTHWISE THEN UNFOLD

2. FOLD CORNERS TO CENTRE

3. FOLD LONG EDGES TO MEET IN THE CENTRE

4. FOLD IN HALF

5. FOLD DOWN WINGS

SPORTS

FUN FACT

A basketball hoop is 10 feet high from the court floor.

FUN FACT

On average, soccer players run as far as 9.5 miles in a match.

FUN FACT

American football was invented in 1882 making it 140 years old.

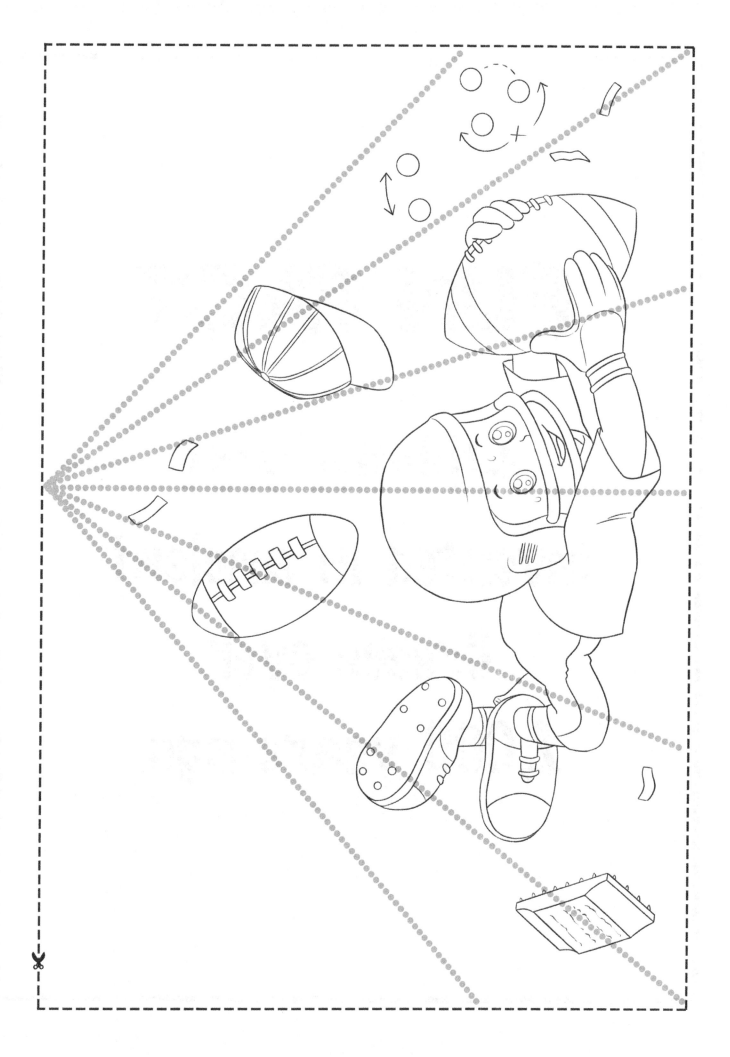

FUN FACT

Athletics was invented in ancient Greece over 2,000 years ago.

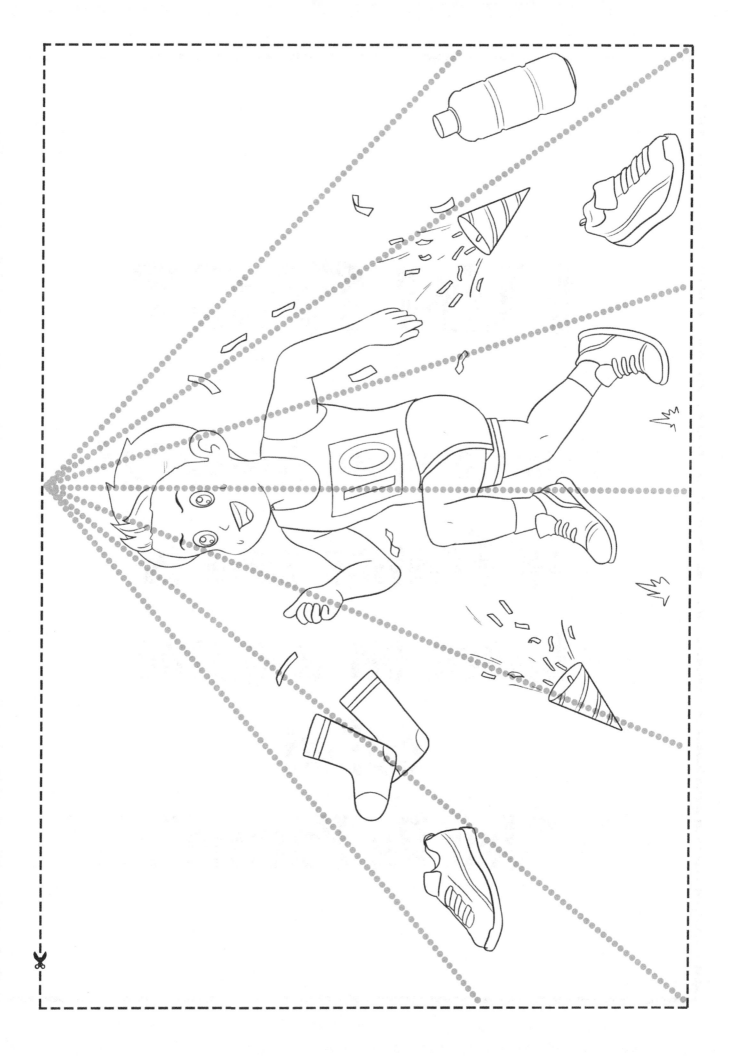

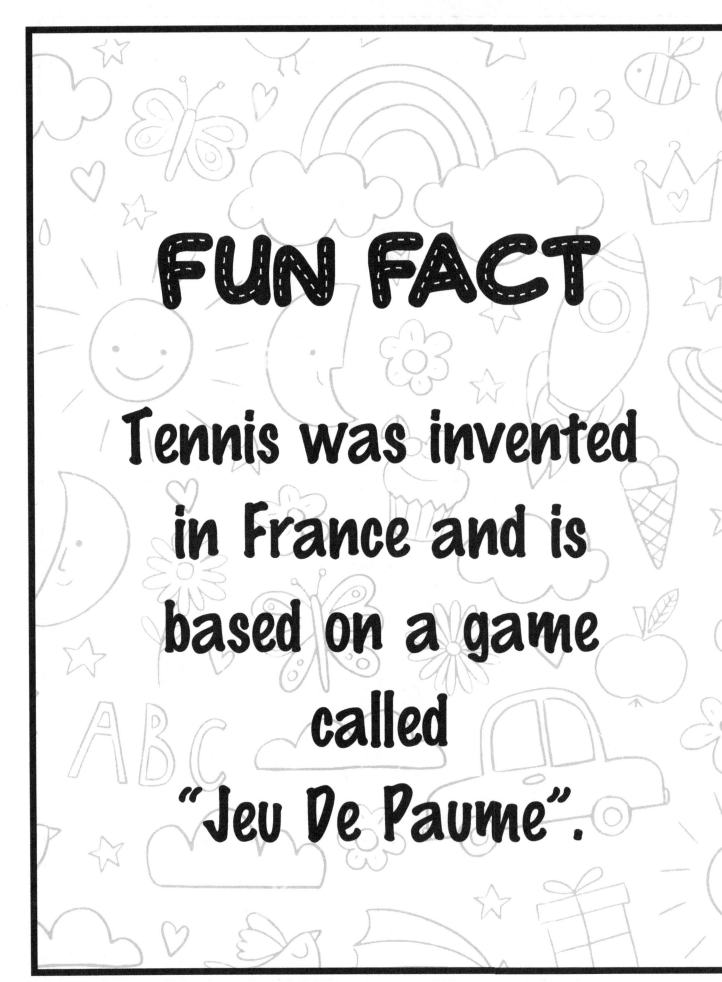

FUN FACT

Tennis was invented in France and is based on a game called "Jeu De Paume".

PLANE #5

1. FOLD IN HALF,
THEN UNFOLD

2. FOLD ANGLED
EDGES IN TO CENTER

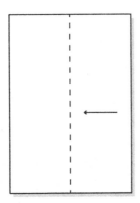

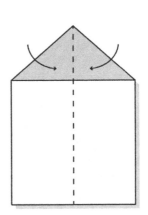

3. FOLD IN
HALF

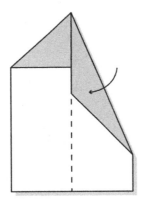

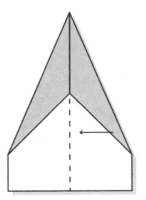

4. FOLD DOWN
WINGS

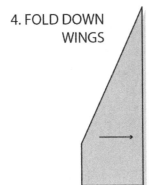

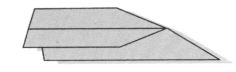

CONSTRUCTION

FUN FACT

Some cranes can lift 22,000 tons. (About 11,000 family cars)

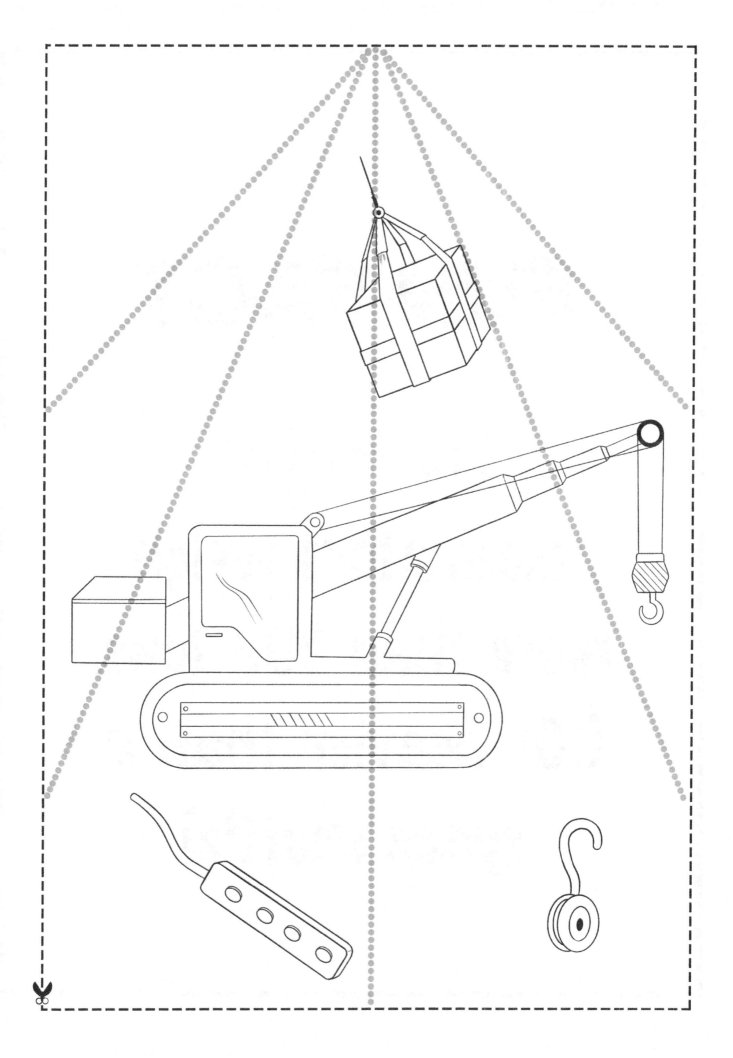

FUN FACT

The largest excavators weigh more than 800 tons. (10x heavier than a space shuttle)

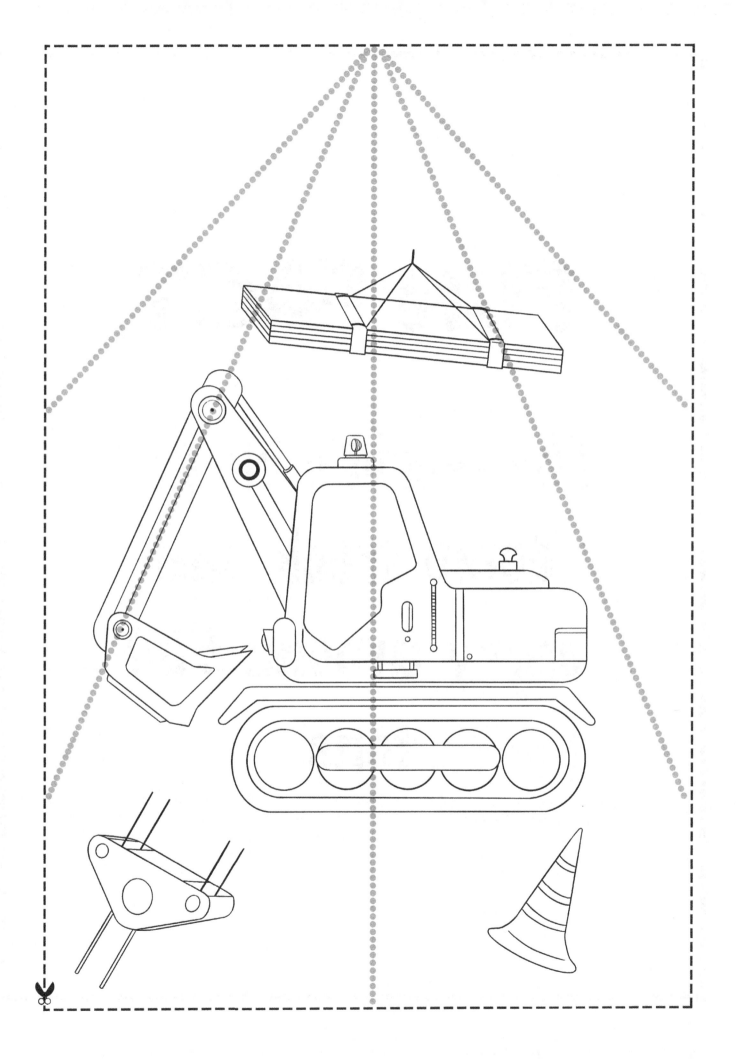

FUN FACT

The world's biggest dump truck can carry around 500 tons.

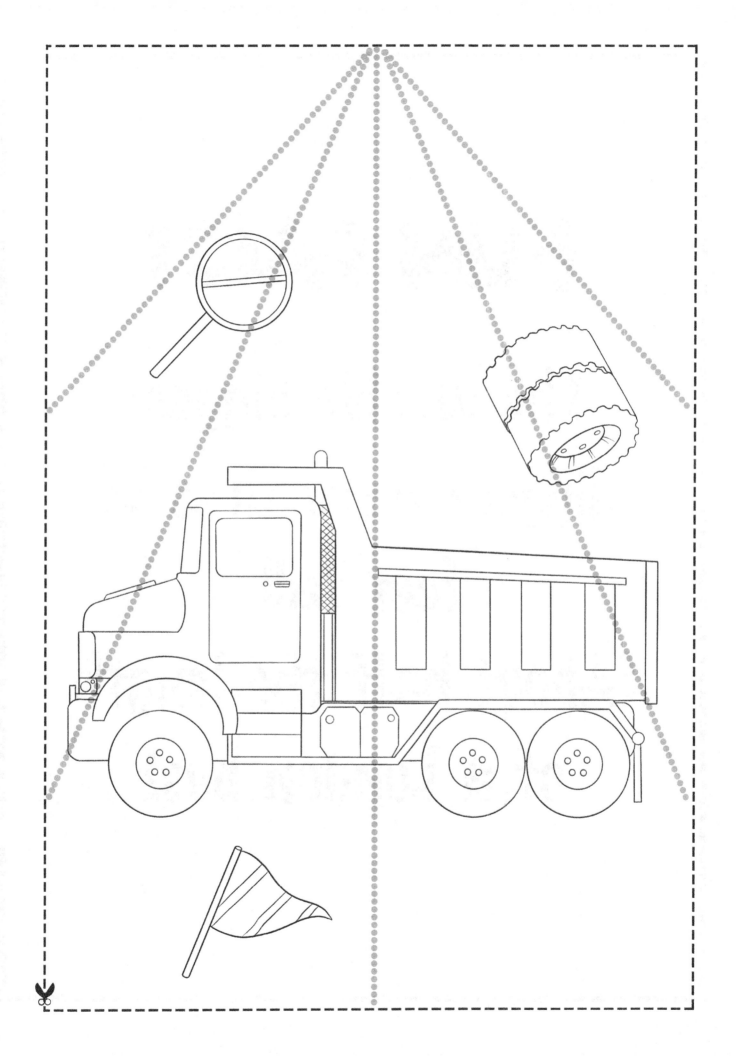

FUN FACT

The worlds biggest diggers have tires 13 feet tall.
(About half the length of a London bus)

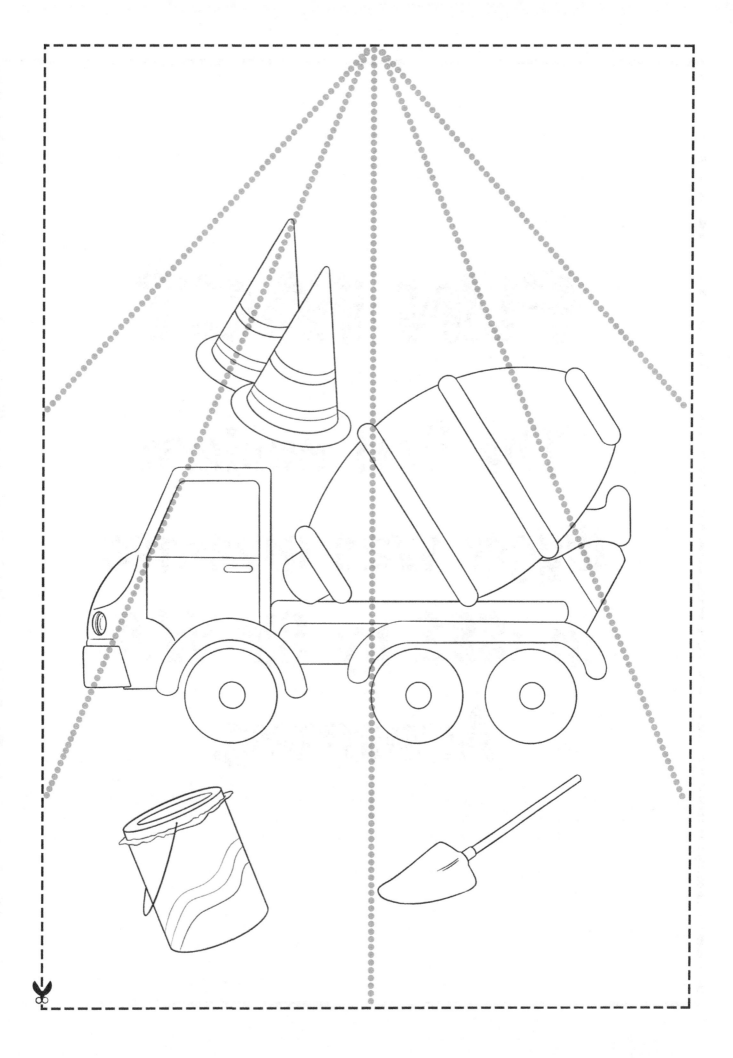

FUN FACT

The first modern digger was invented in 1882 by Sir W.G Armstrong.

Made in the USA
Monee, IL
19 October 2023

44875277R00037